Castles

greyscale coloring book

by

Tabz Jones

©TabzJones

Books by Tabz Jones

Digital Landscape Adult Coloring Book

Fantasy Art Mini Adult Coloring Book

Sun and Sand Adult Coloring Book

Gothic Fairy Dream Journal

Rockabilly Roses Journal

Dark Matter Adult Coloring Book

Gothic Girls Adult Coloring Book Volumes 1-7

Dangerous Curves Adult Coloring Book

Fantasy Men Adult Coloring Book

Harlequinn Pastel Fantasy Dream Journal

Gothiscopic Kaleidoscopes Coloring Book

Darling Dolls

Fantastic Creatures

Gothic Girls Art Book

Rose Cross Dream Journal

Reflections Vampire Poetry

Steampunk Adult Coloring Book

Angelic Book of Shadows

Fantastic Creatures

Fantasy Fae Adult Coloring Book

Fractal Art Adult Coloring Book Volumes 1-2

In Loving Memory Churchyard Adult Coloring Book

Fantasy Art Adult Coloring Book Volumes 1-2

Doodle Monsters Adult Coloring Book

Summer Flowers Adult Coloring Book

Skullz Adult Coloring Book Volumes 1-2

Dark Fantasy Adult Coloring Book Volumes 1-3

Classic Swears Adult Coloring Book Standard and Mini Editions

Statuesque Adult Coloring Book

Copyright © 2016 by Tabz Jones

All rights reserved. This book or any portion thereof

may not be reproduced or used in any manner whatsoever

without the express written permission of the author

except for the use of brief quotations in a book review.

Printed in the United States of America

First Printing, 2016

ISBN-13: 978-1539831808

ISBN-10: 1539831809

Tabz Jones

PO BOX 2137

Alma AR 72921

www.gothictoggs.net

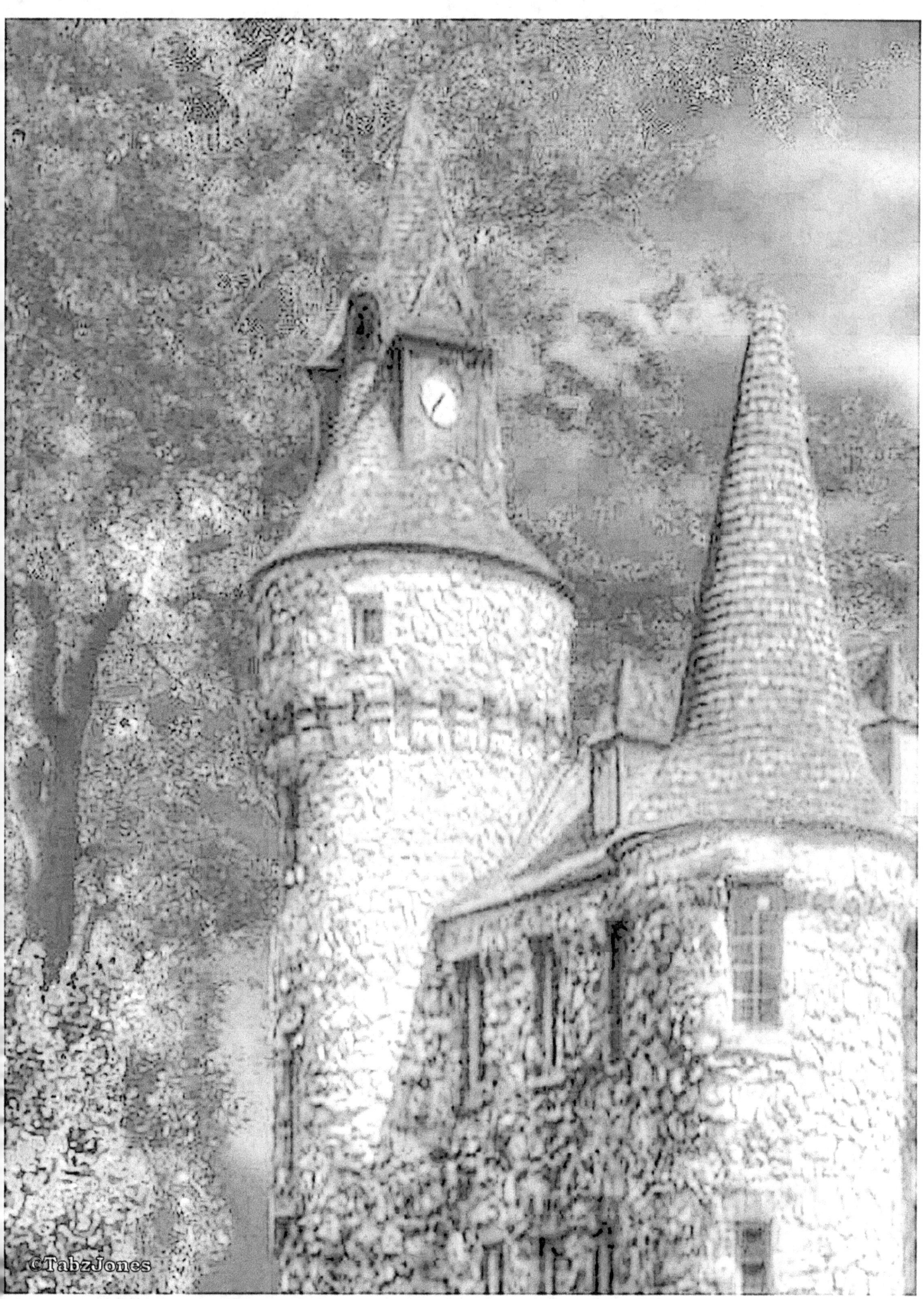

©TabzJones

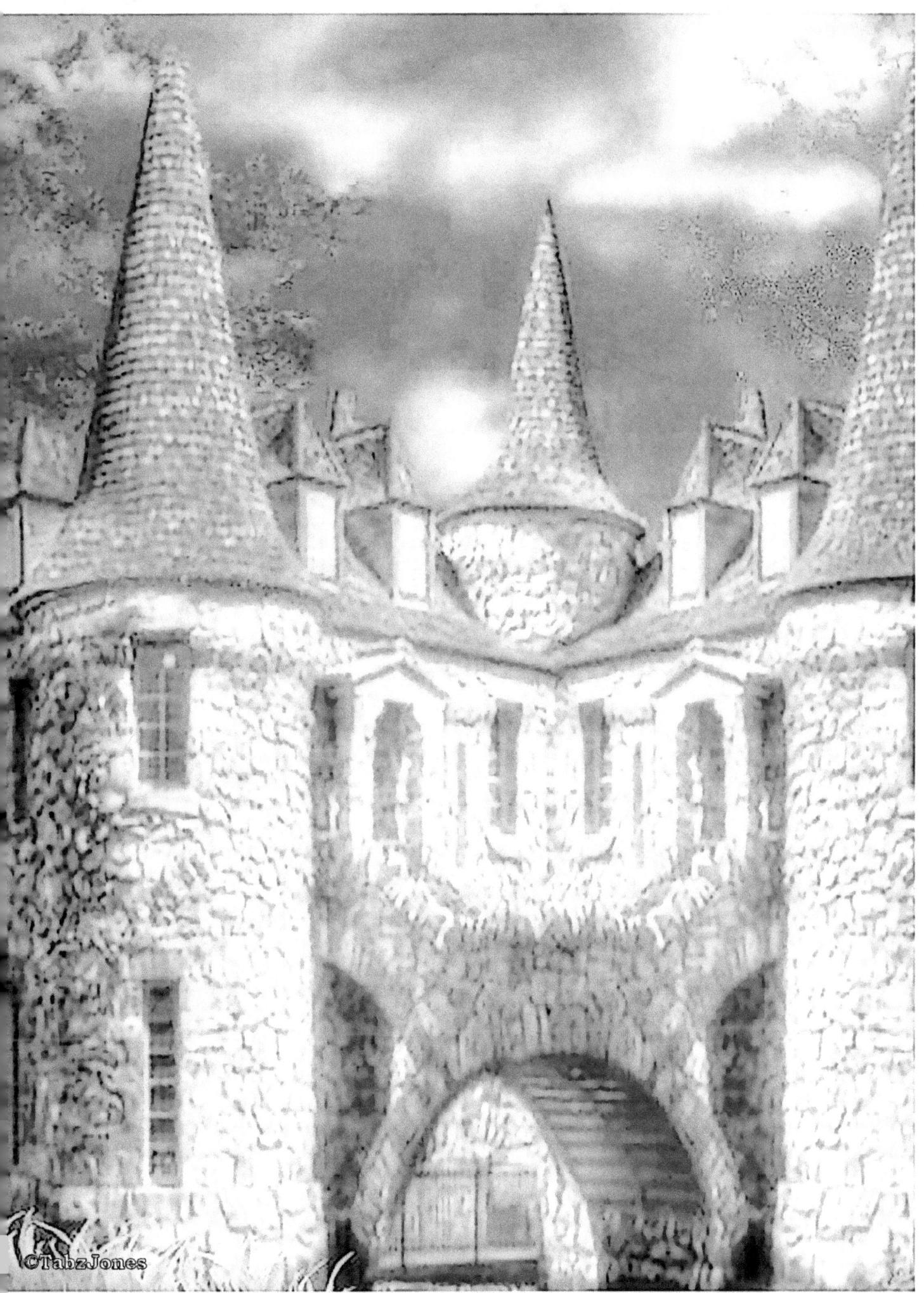

©TabzJones

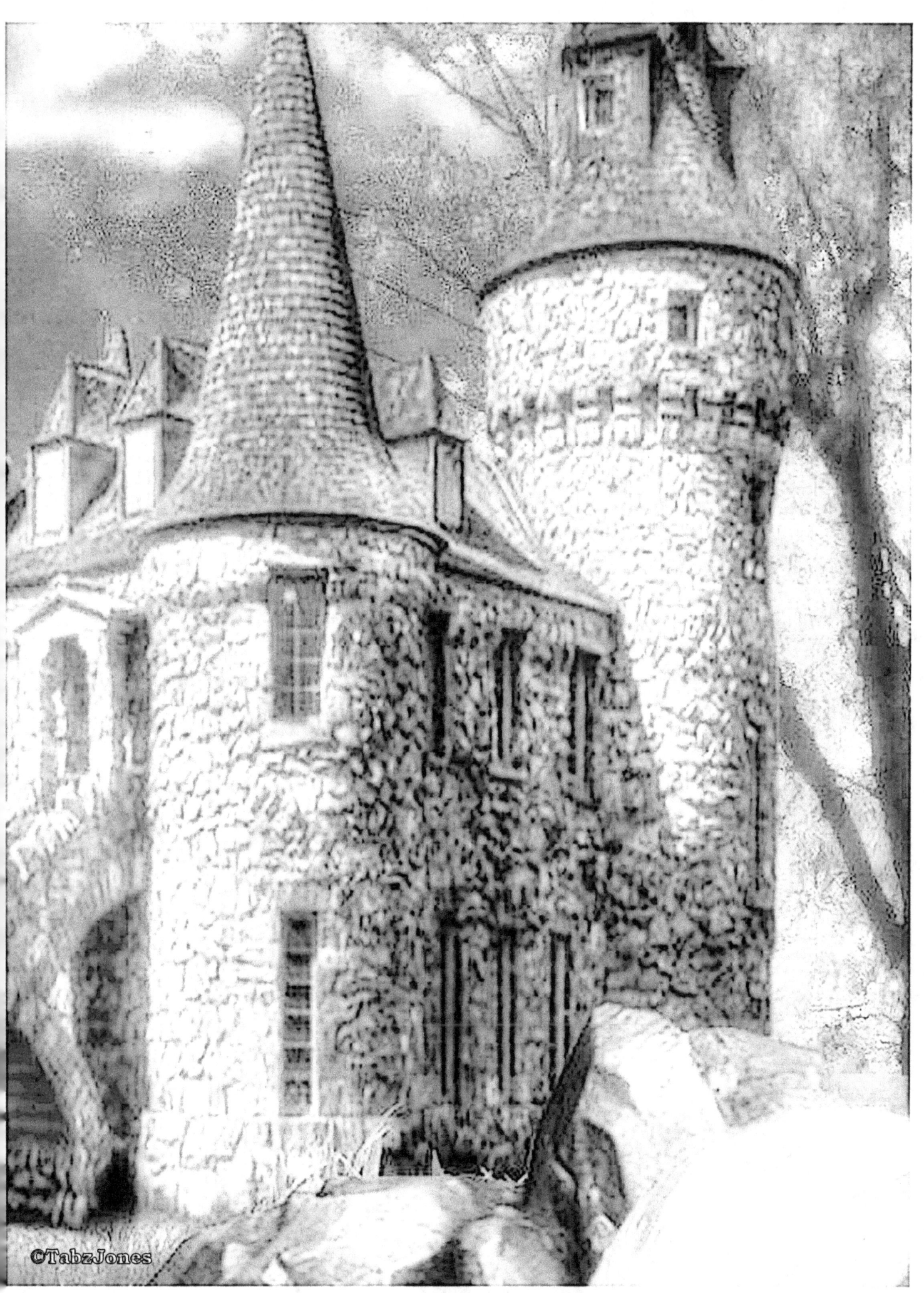

©TabzJones

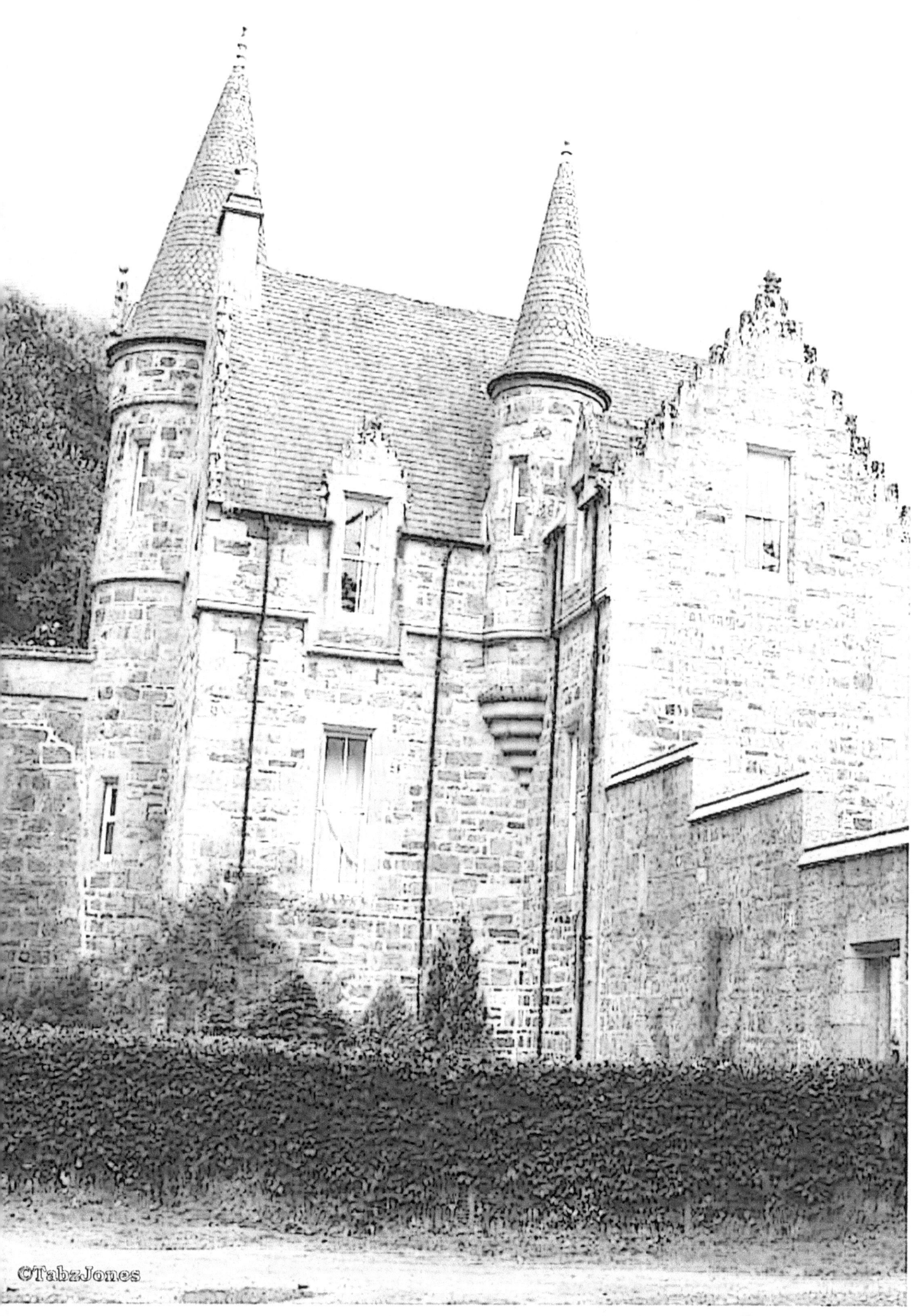

©TabzJones

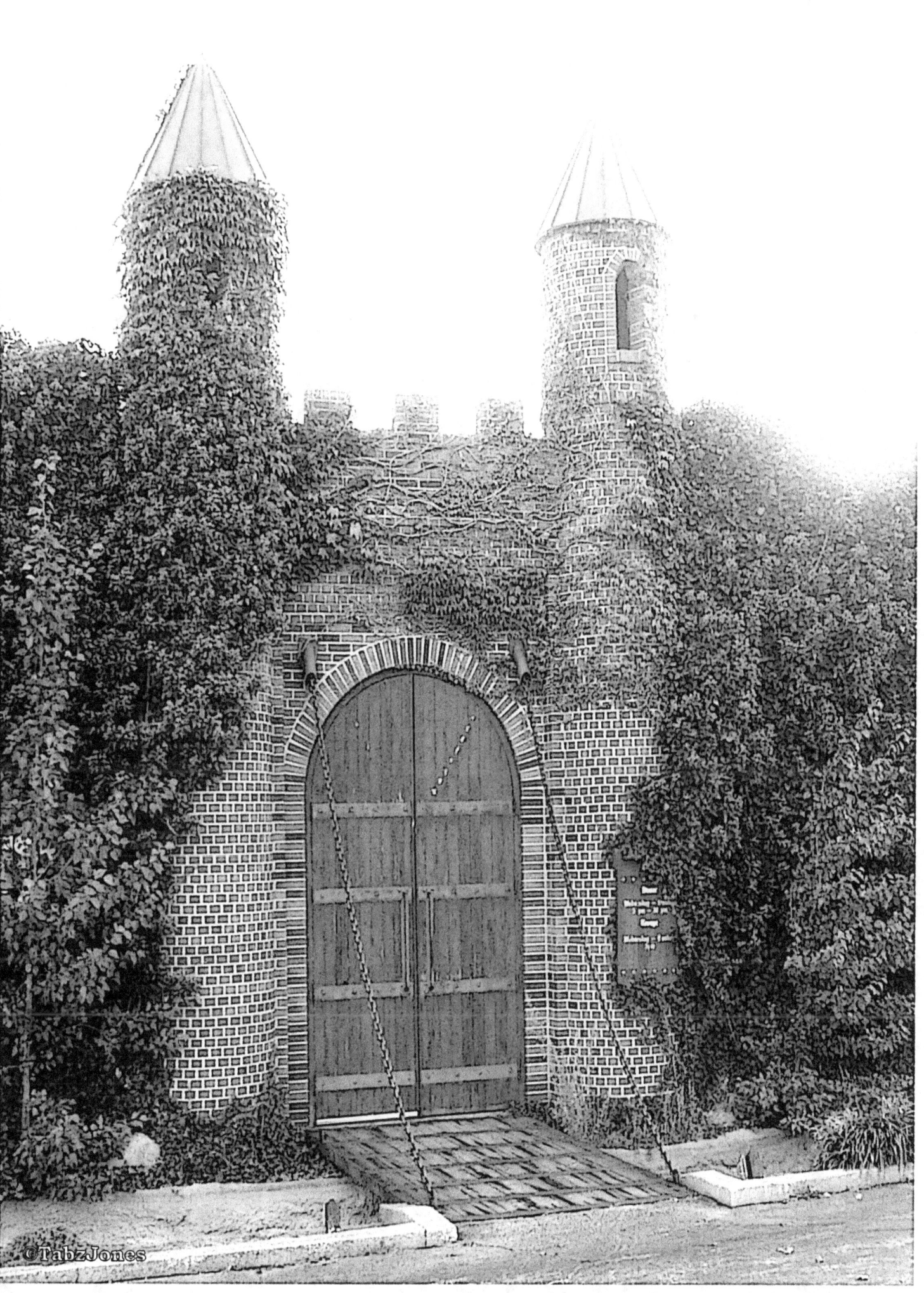

©TabzJones

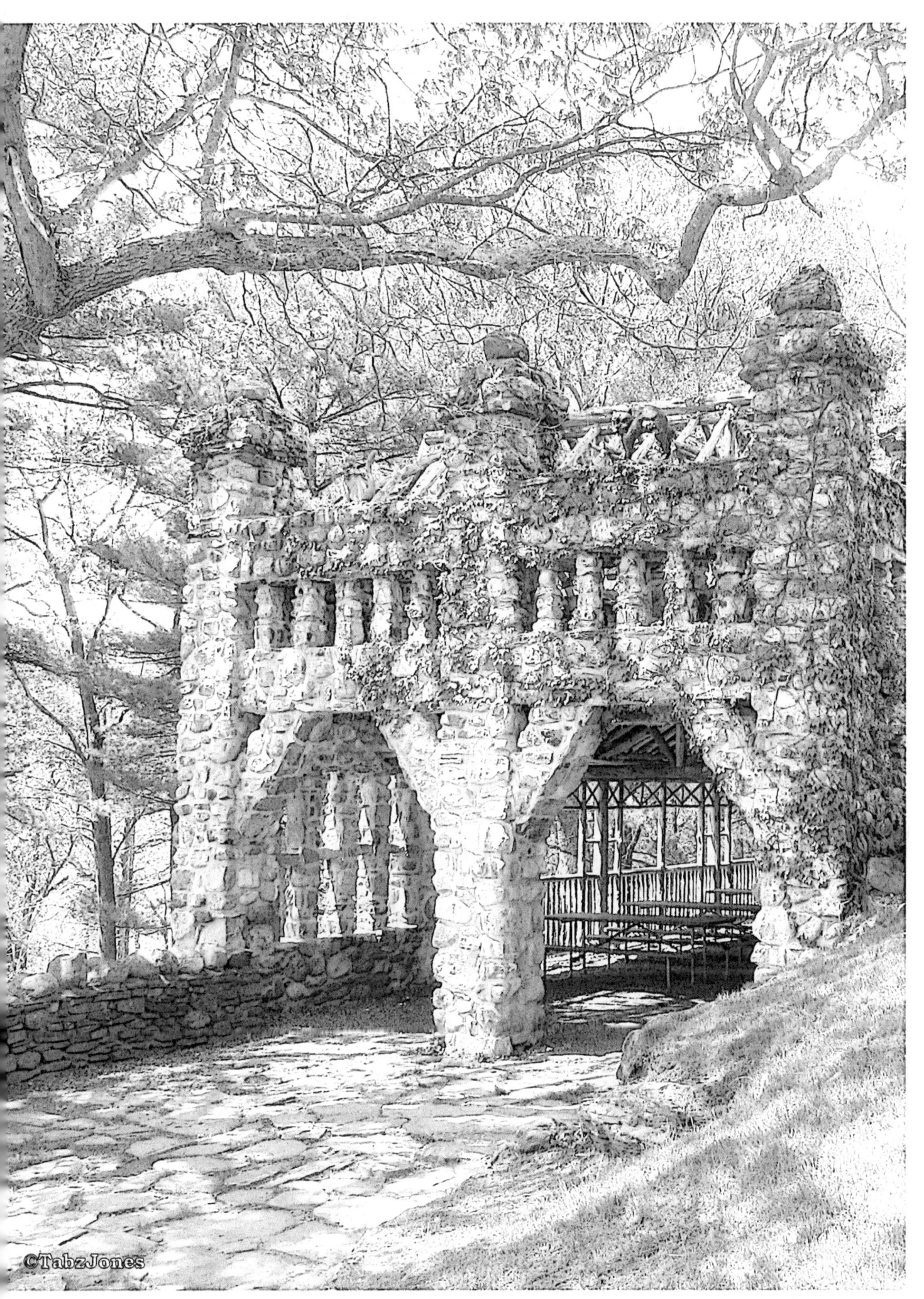
©TabzJones

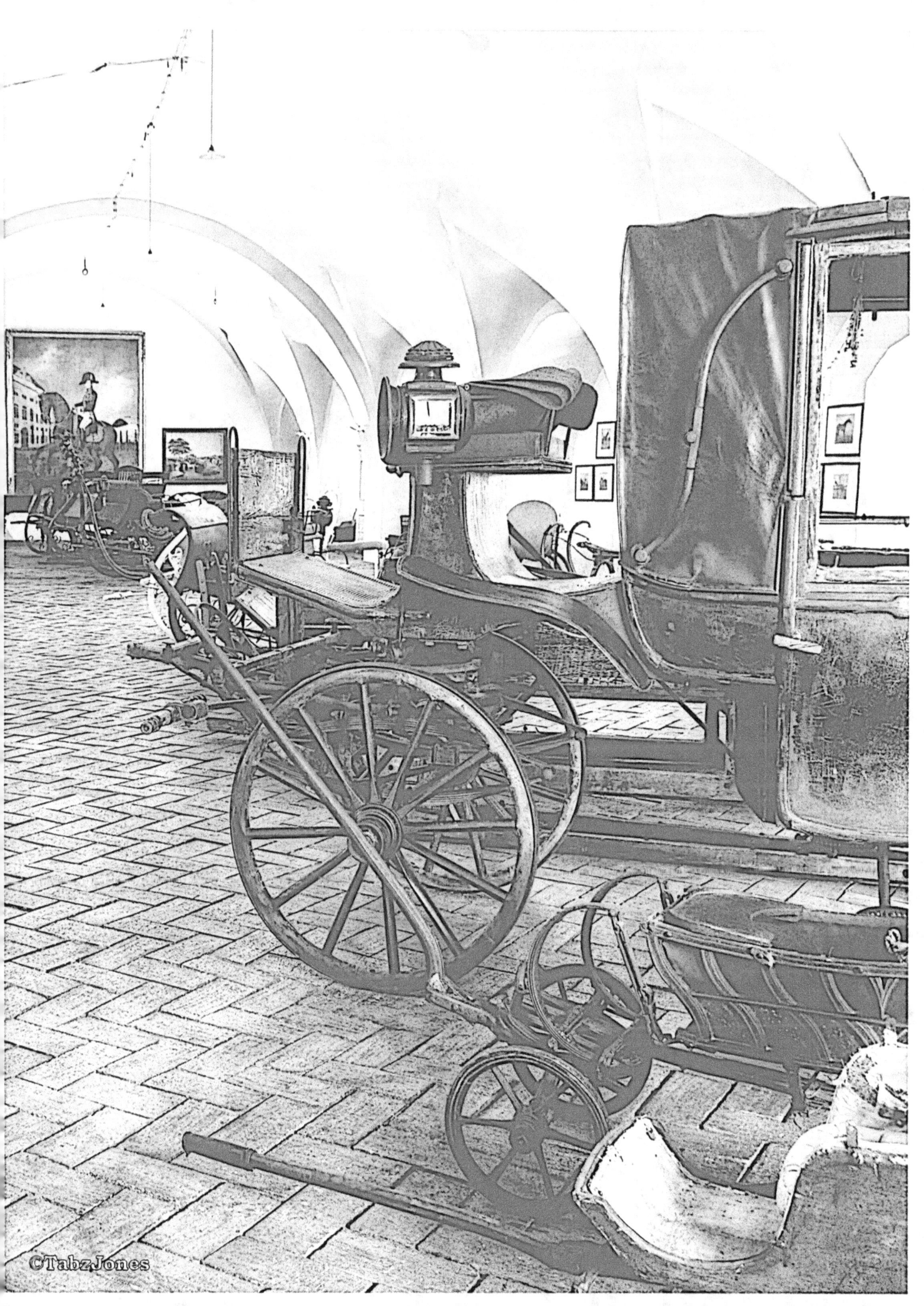

©TabzJones

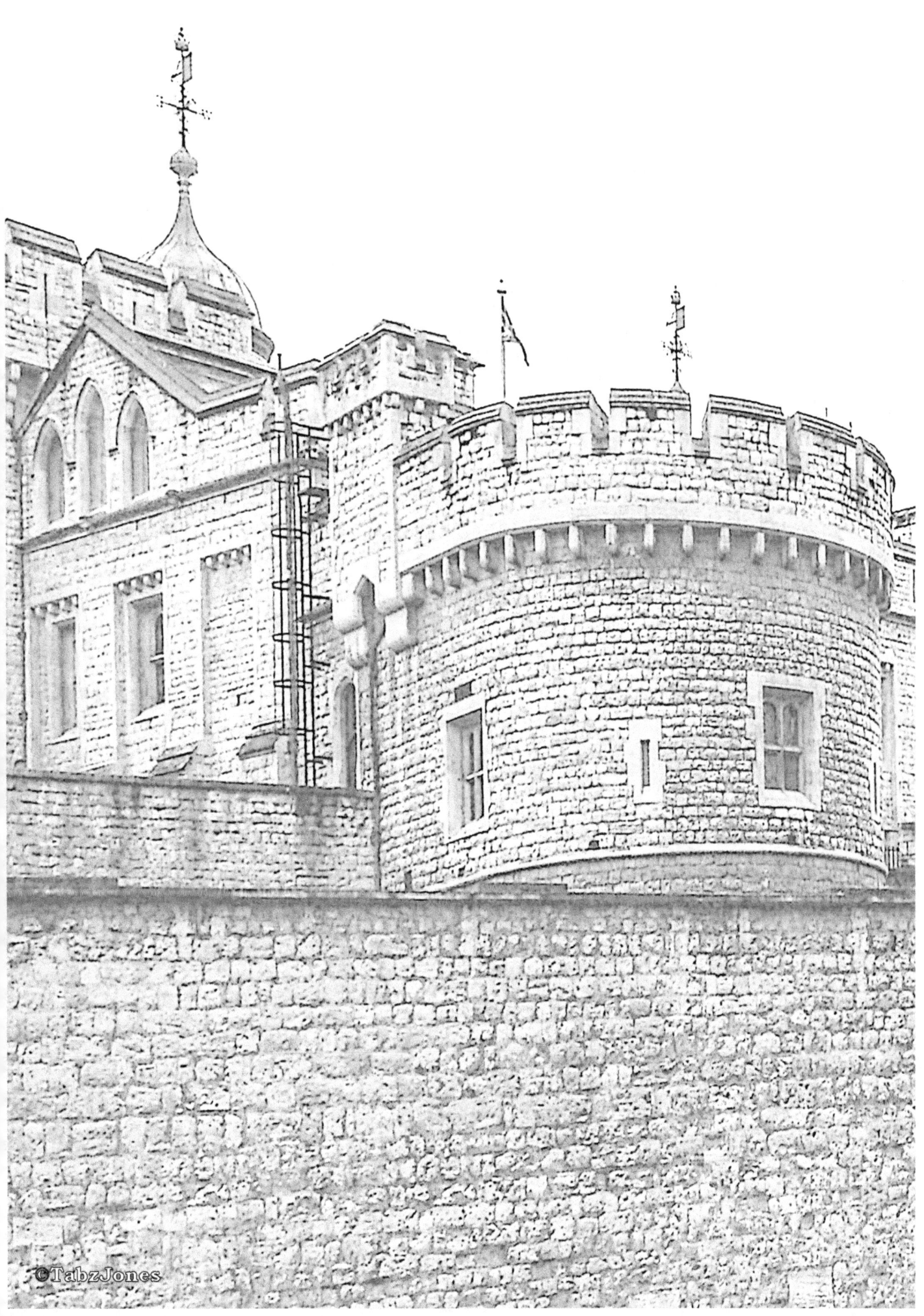
©TabzJones

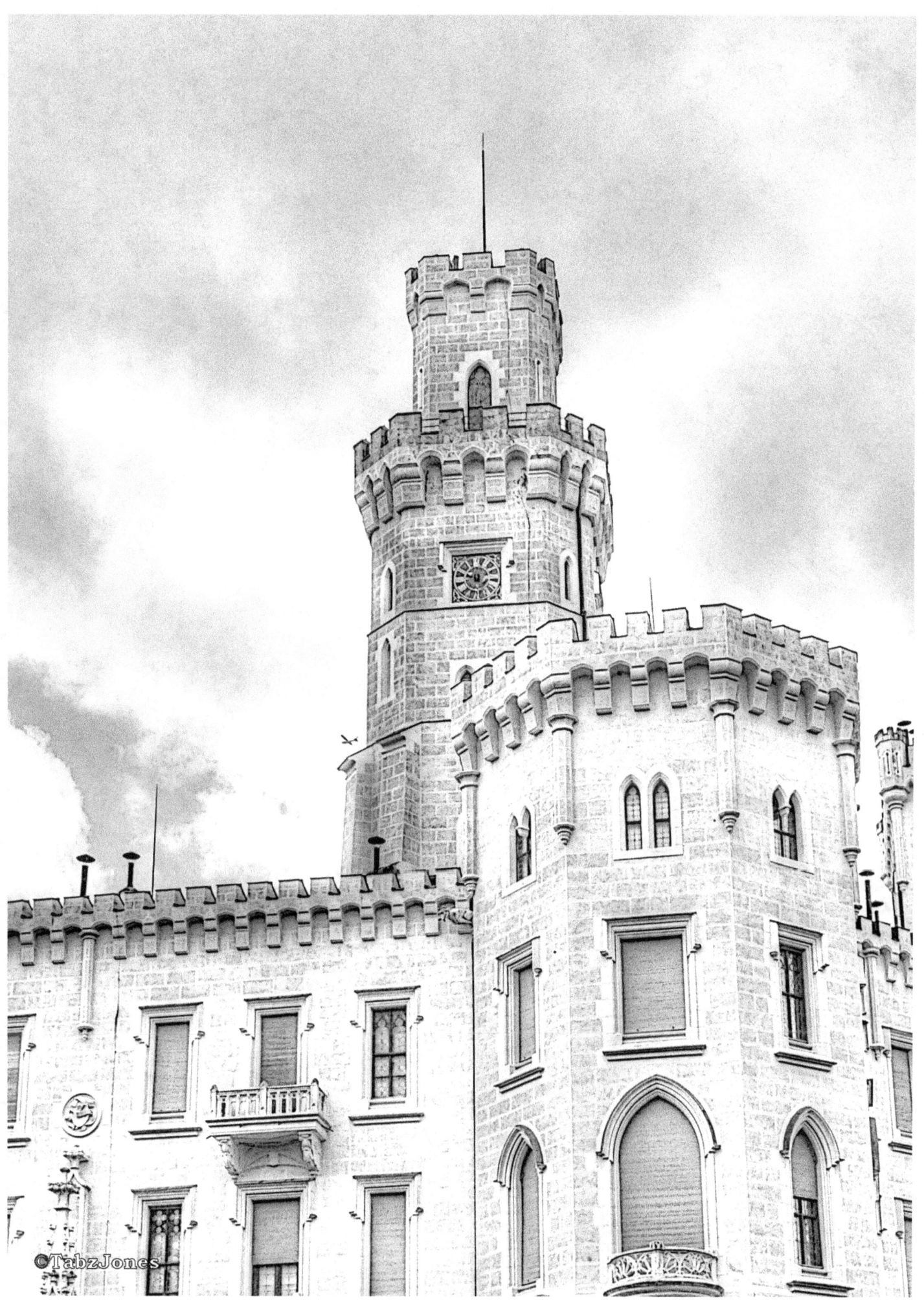

©TabzJones

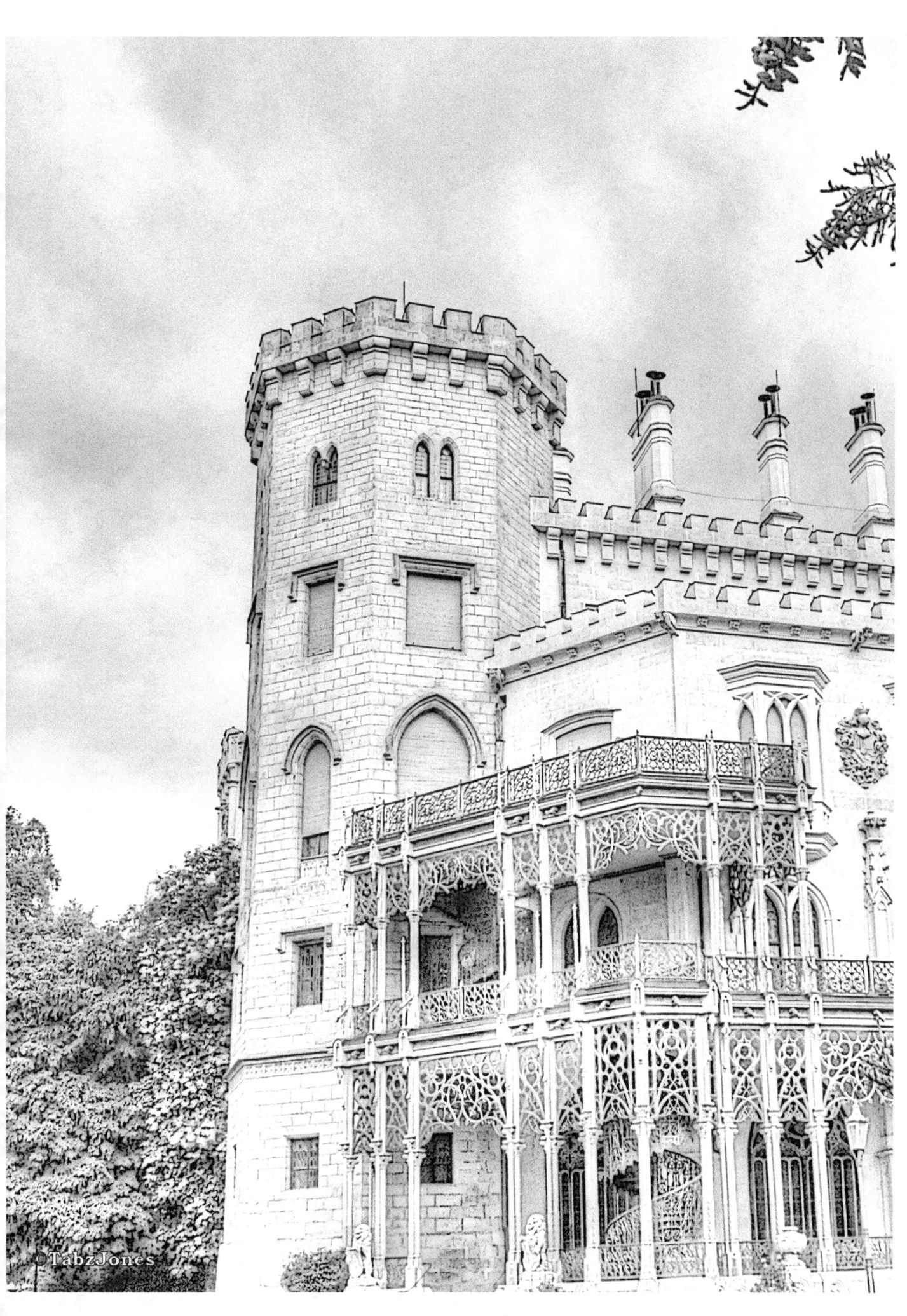
©TabzJones

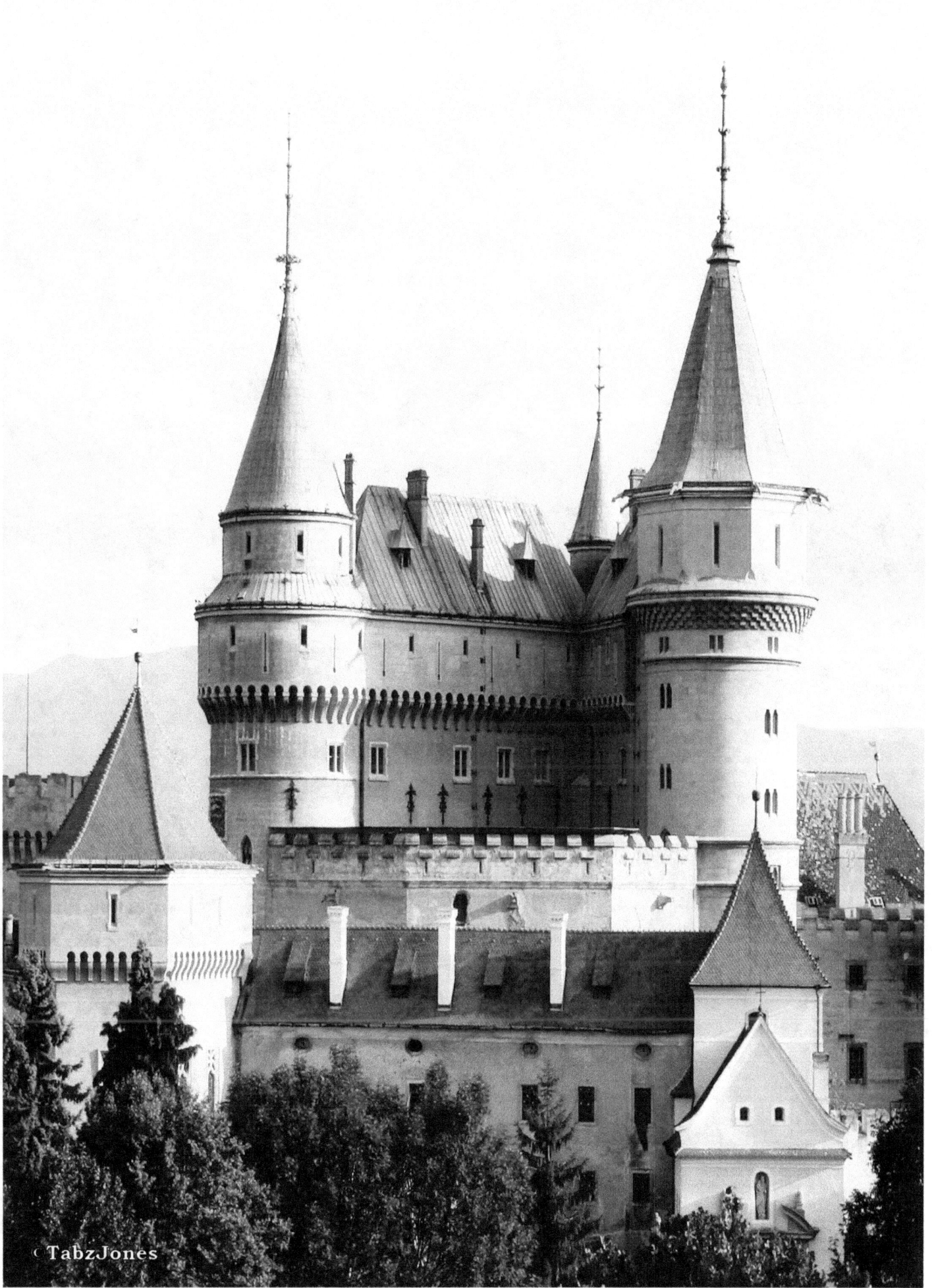

© TabzJones

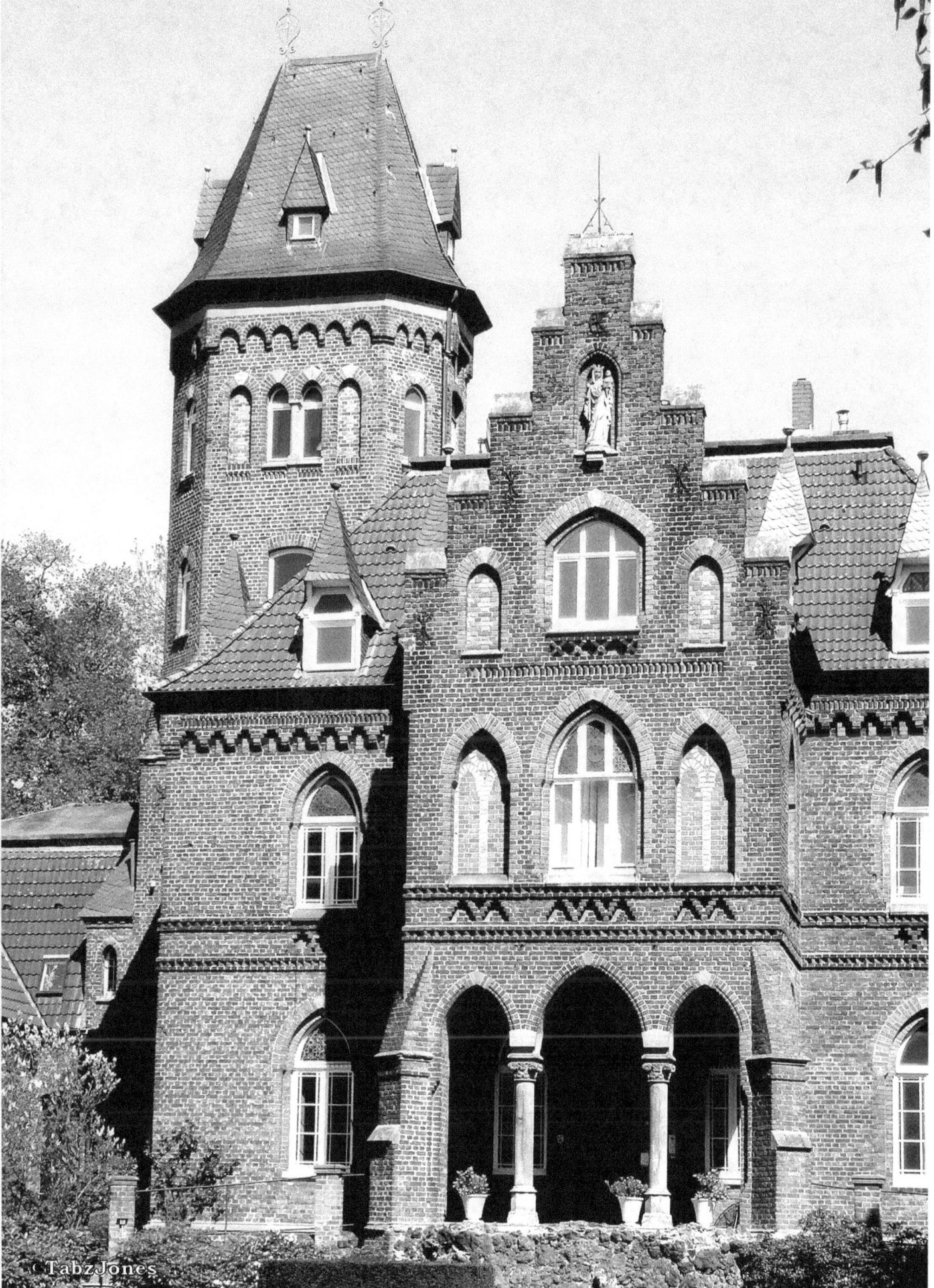

©TabzJones

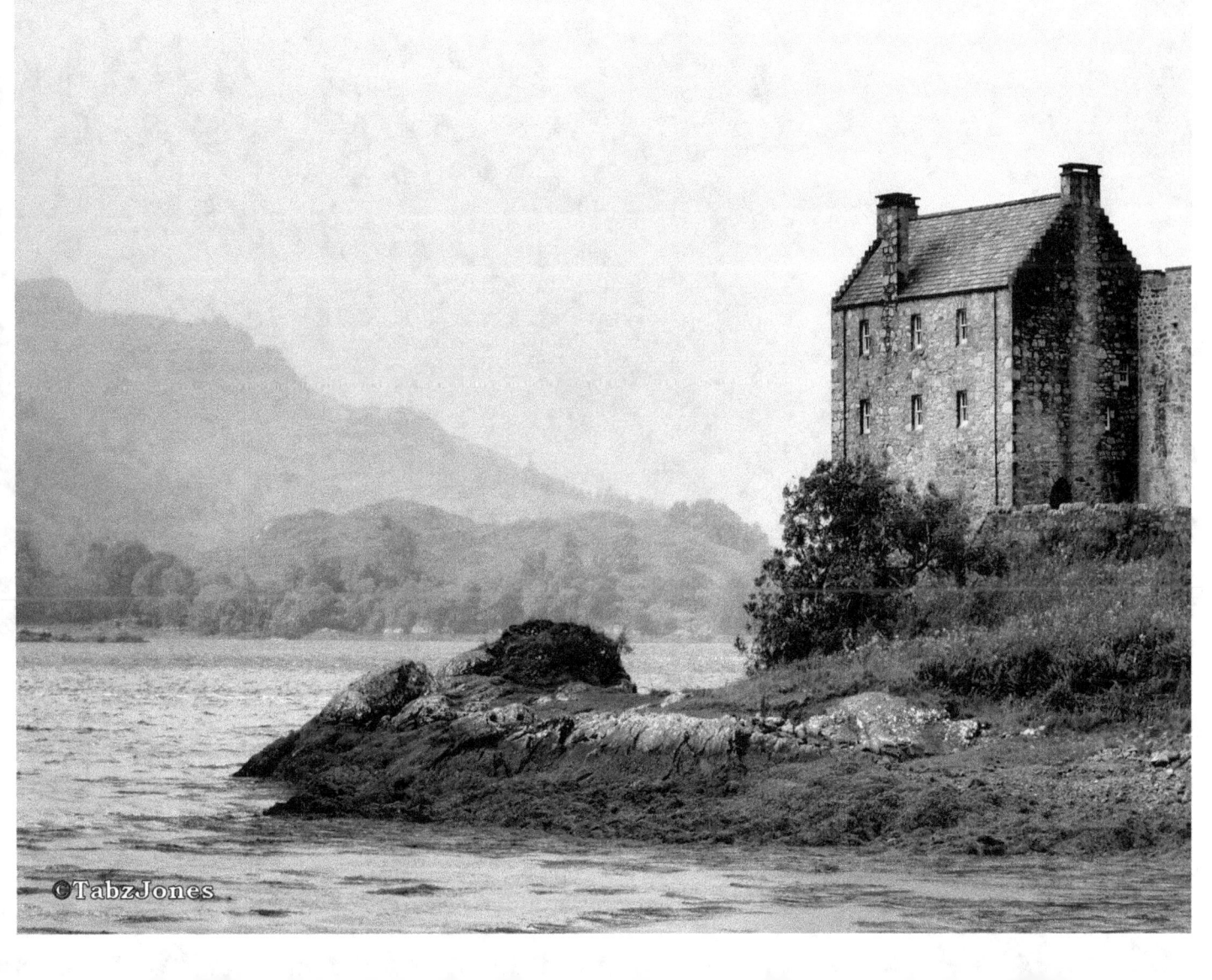

©TabzJones

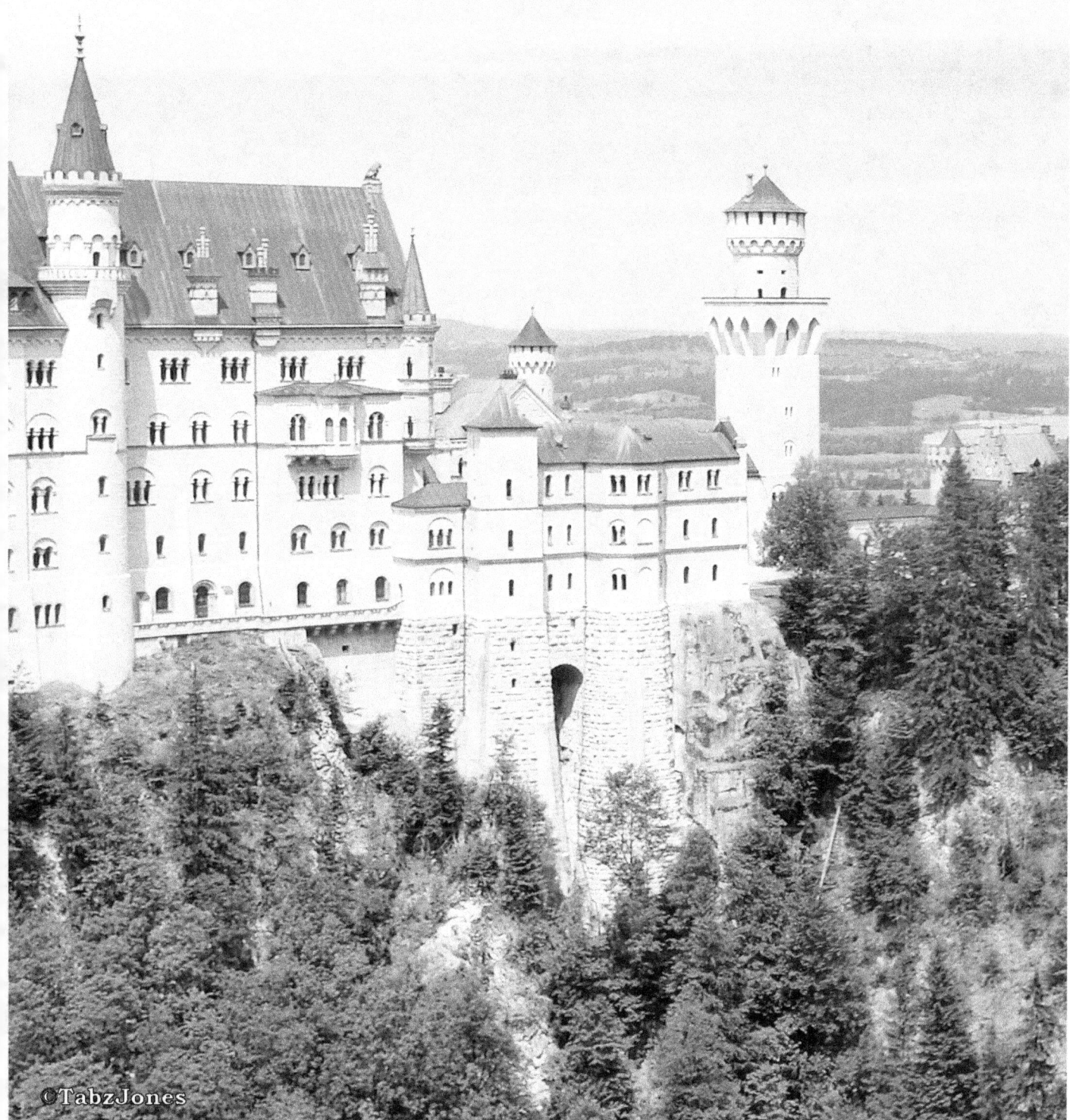

©TabzJones

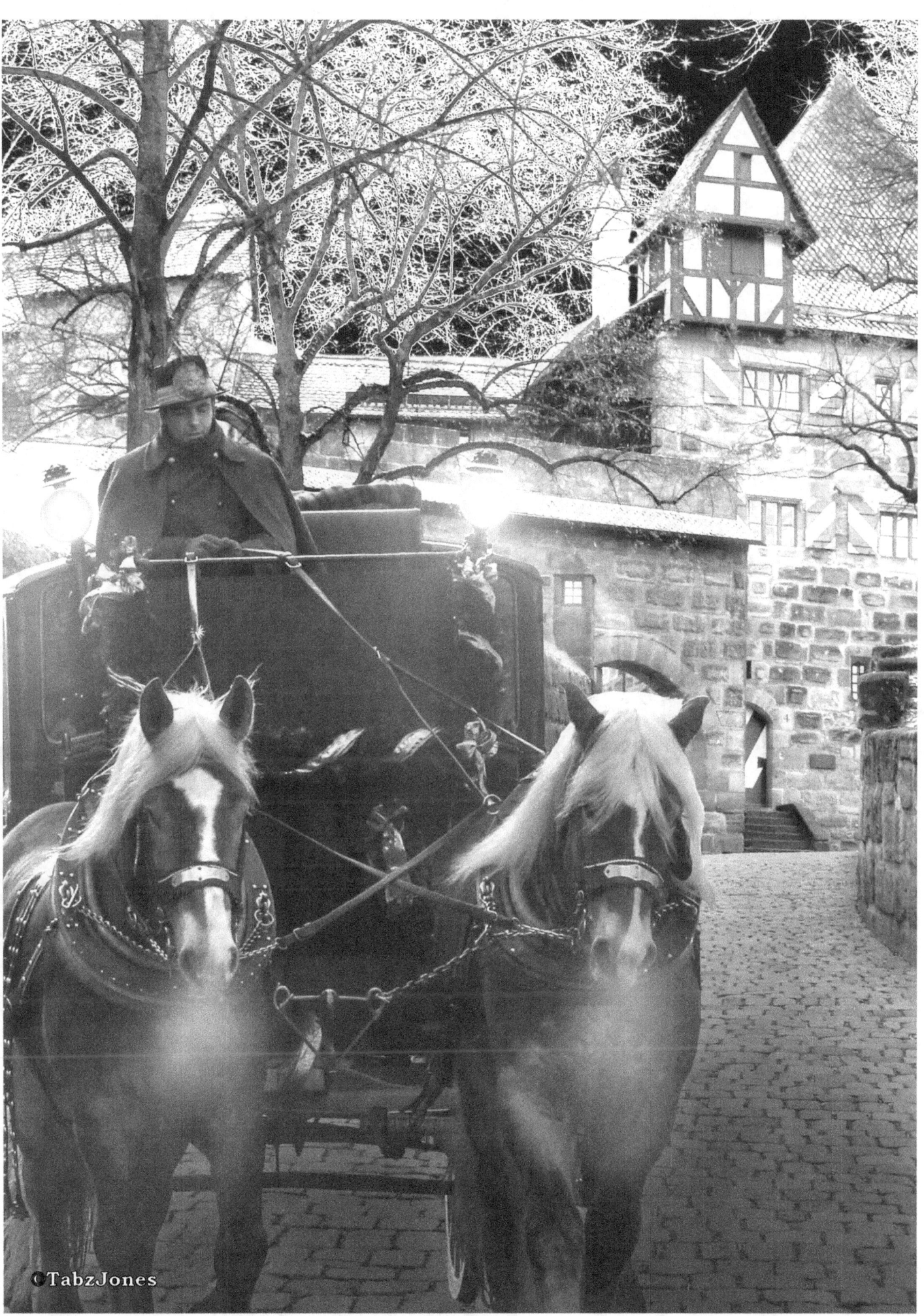
©TabzJones

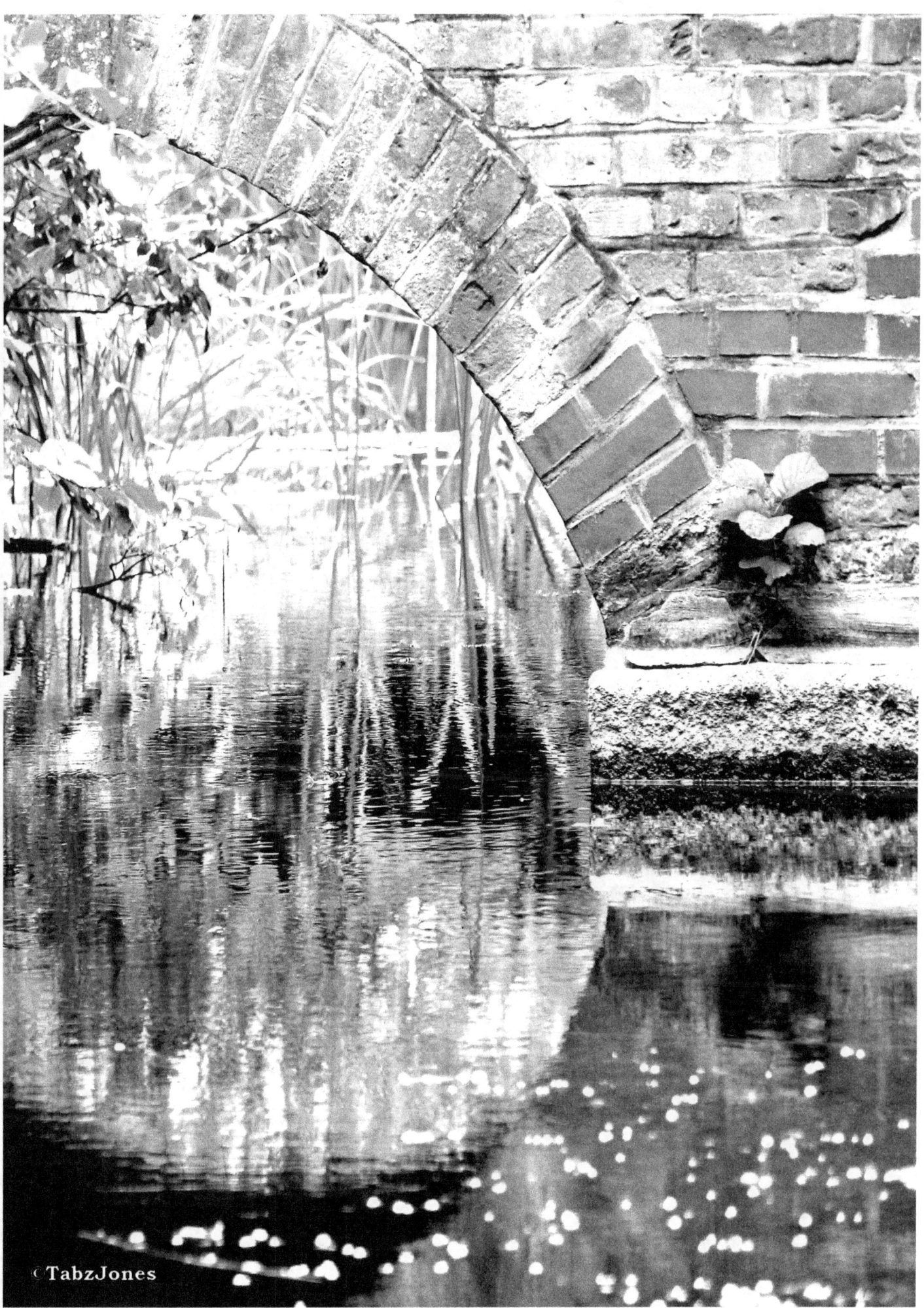
©TabzJones

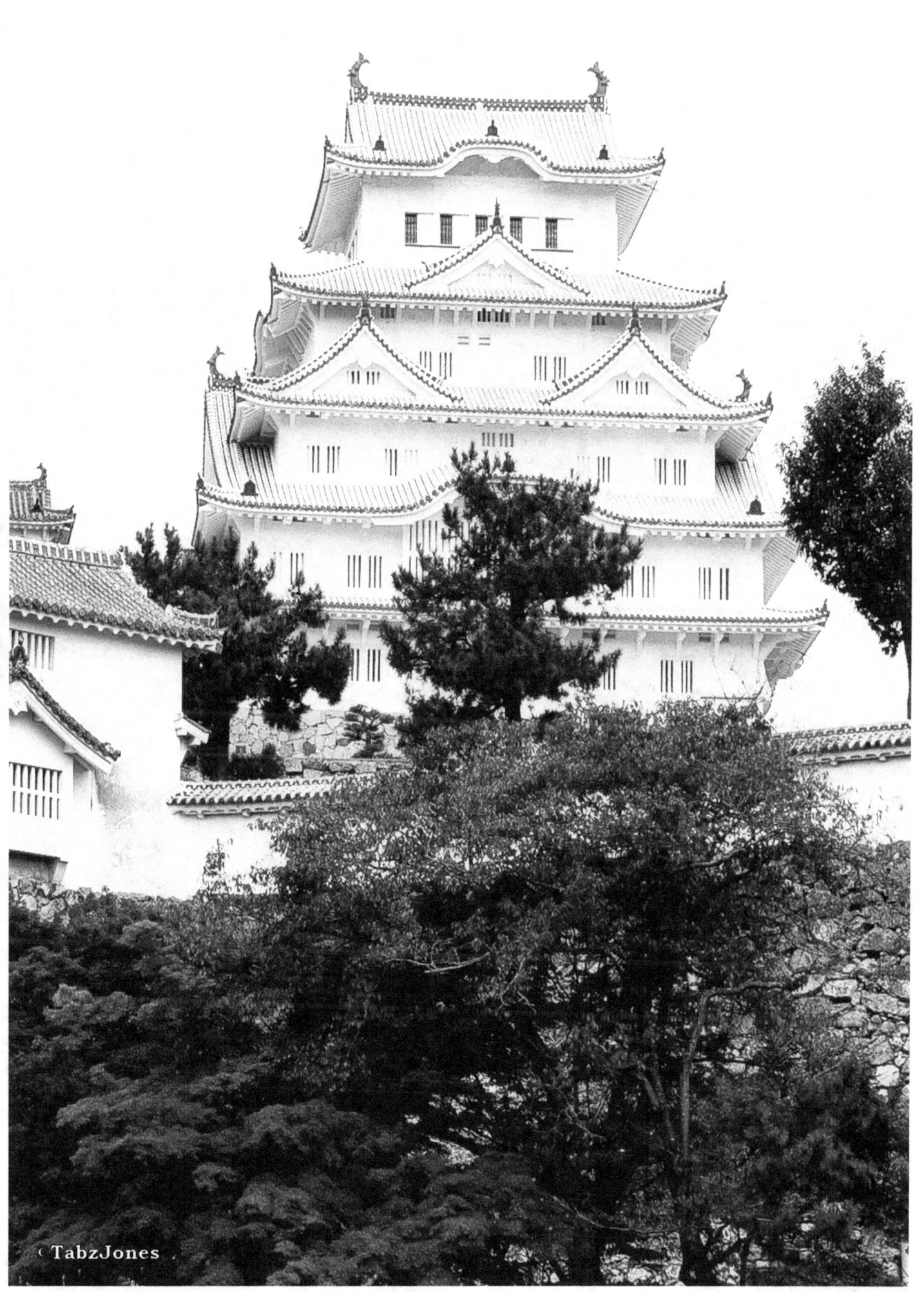

© TabzJones

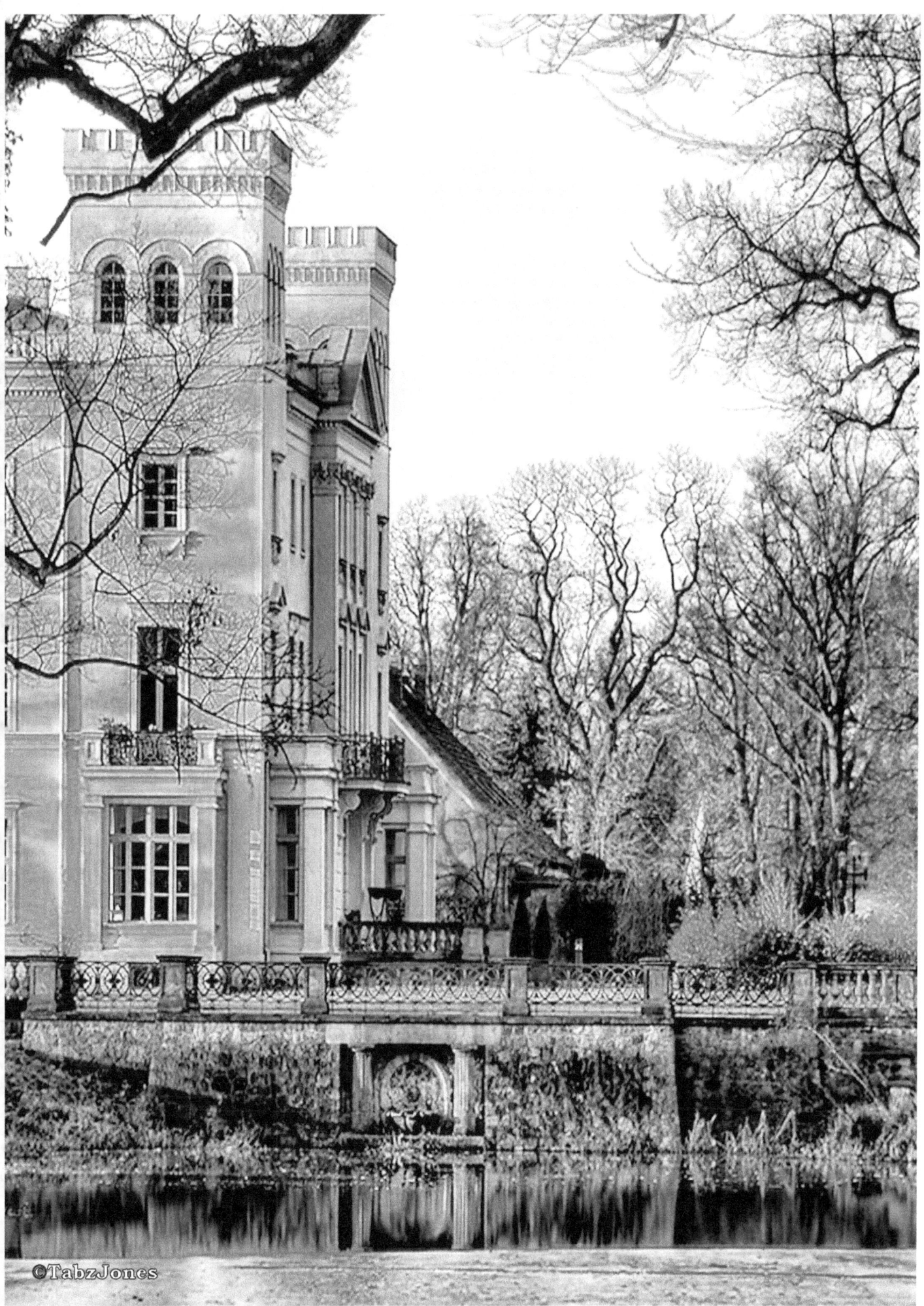

©TabzJones

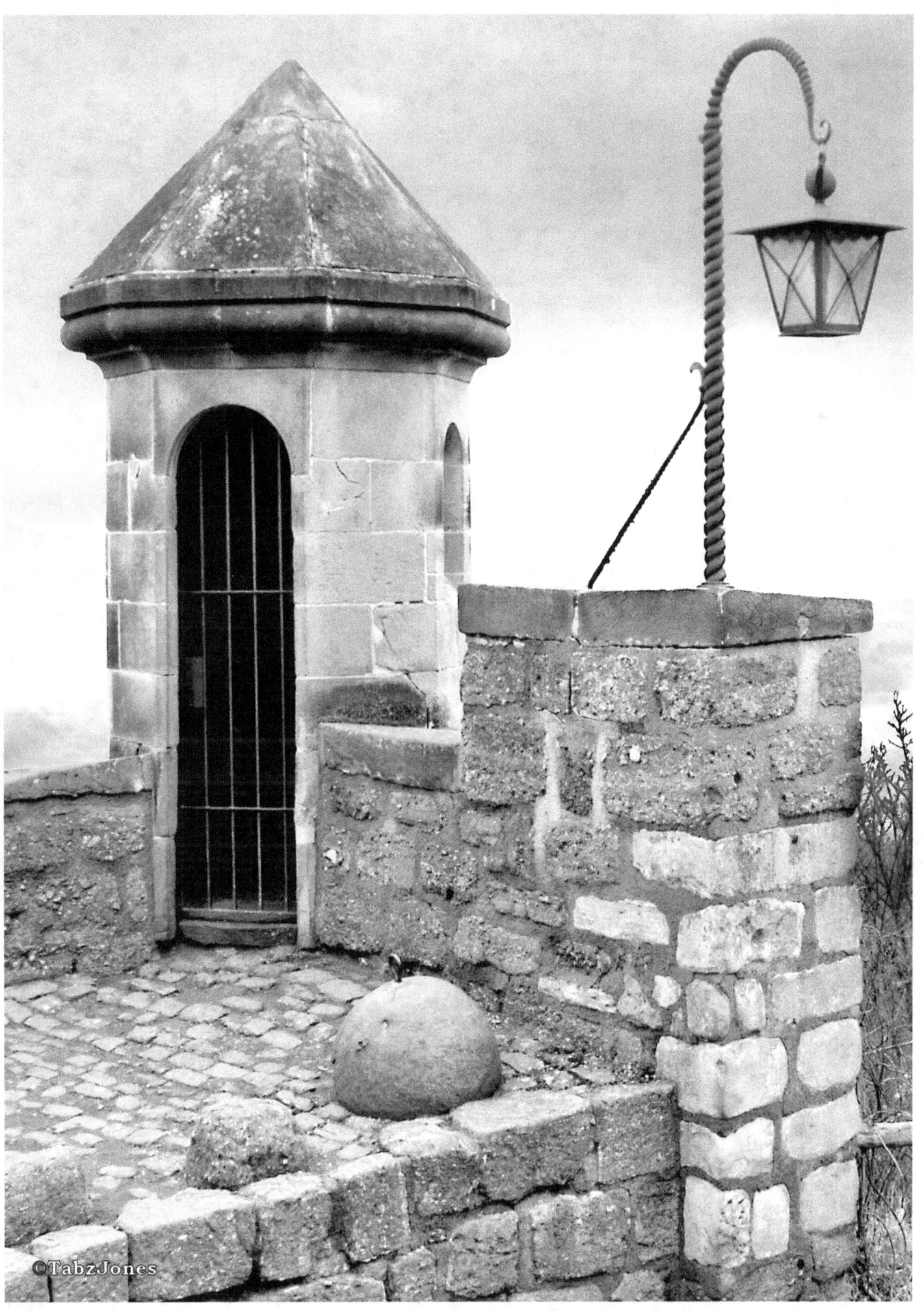

©TabzJones

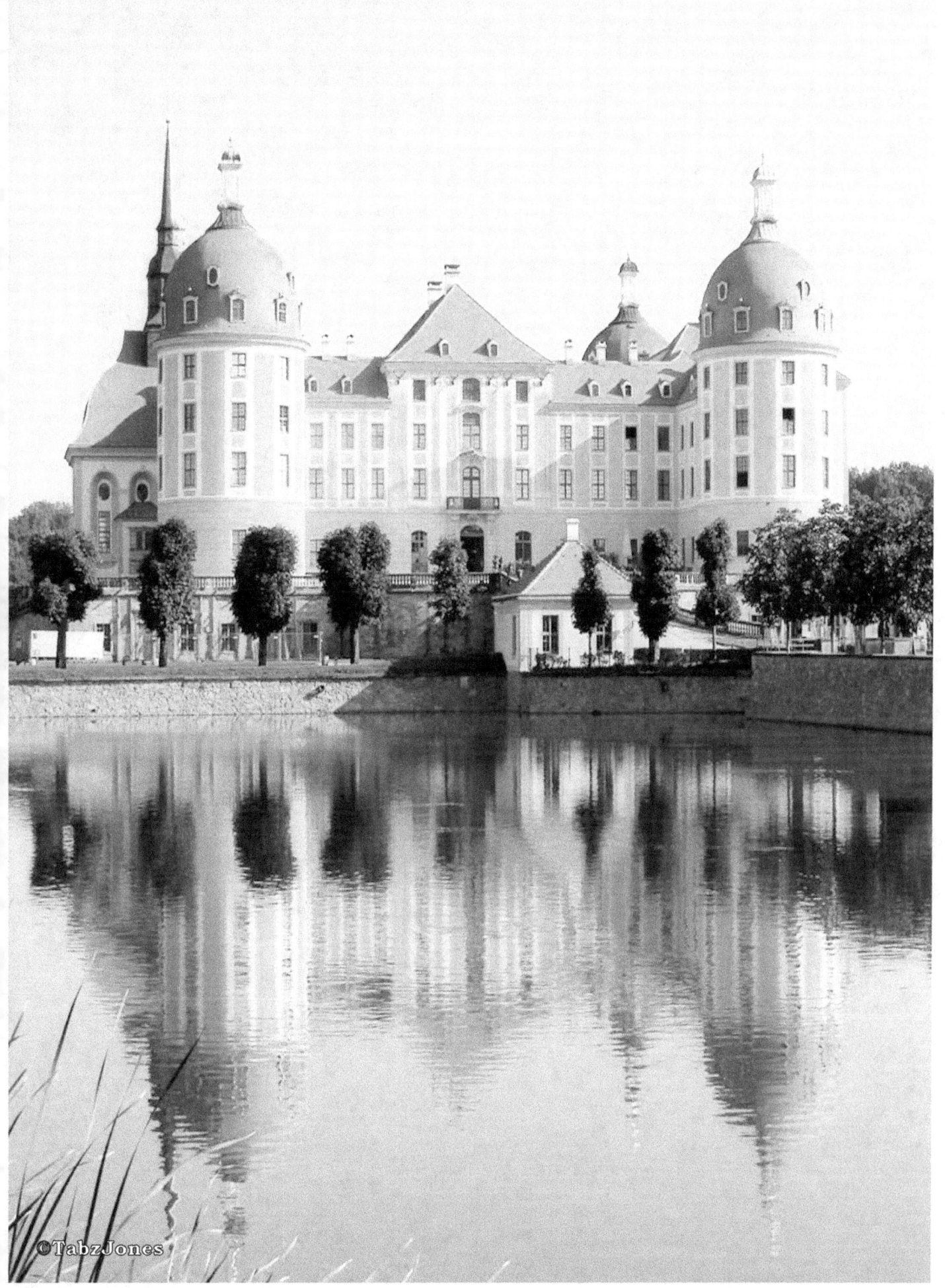

©TabzJones

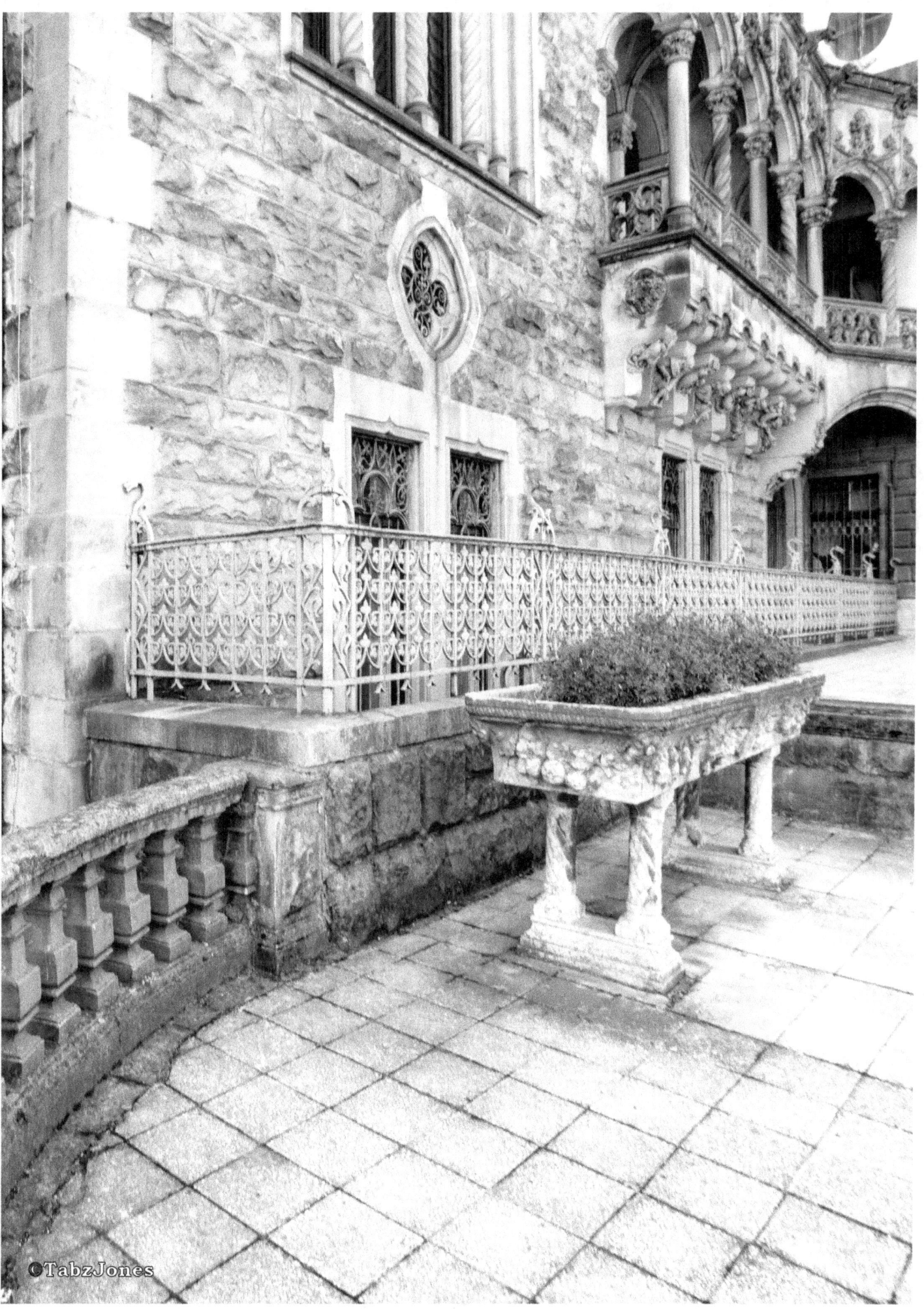

©TabzJones

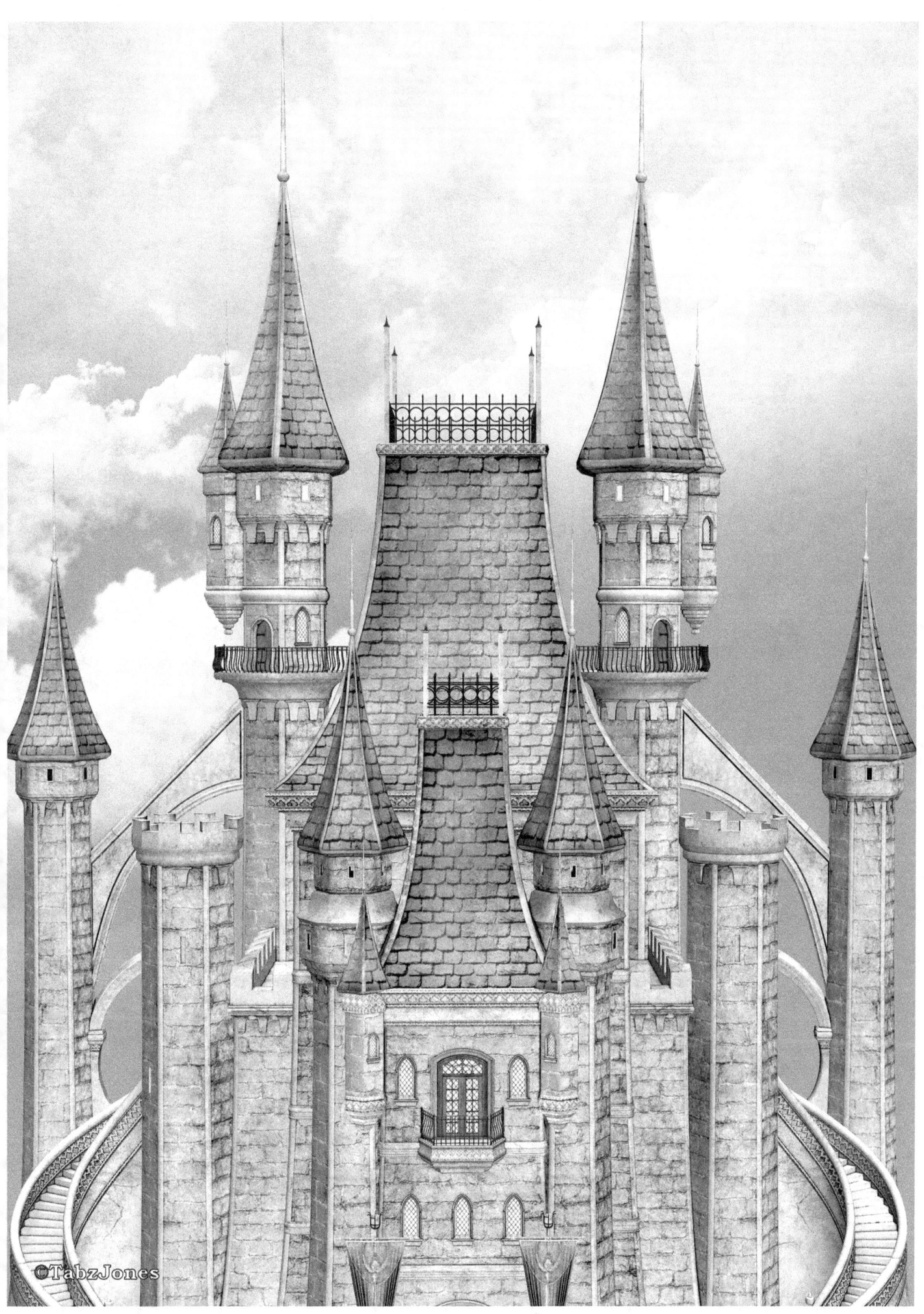
©TabzJones

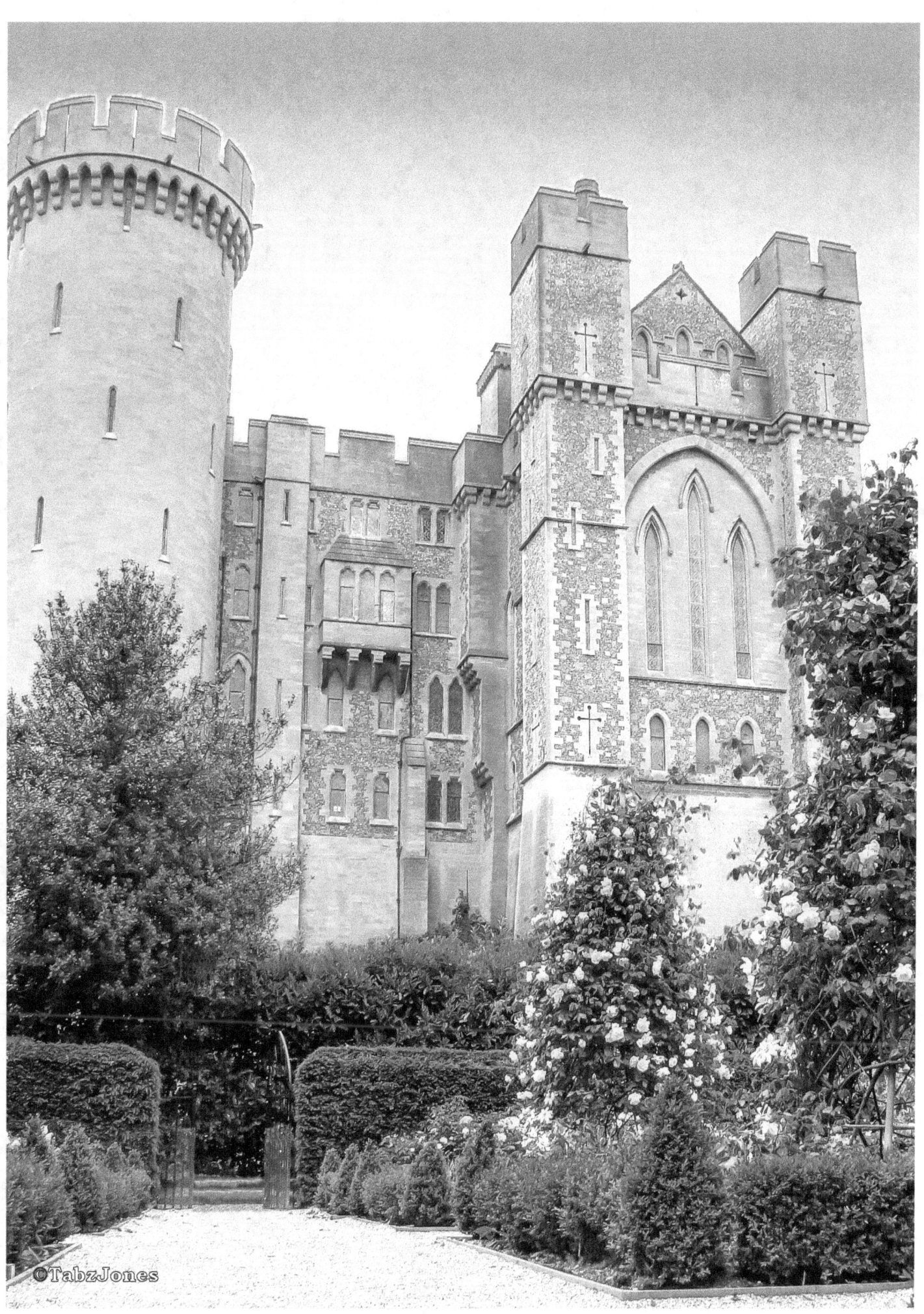
©TabzJones

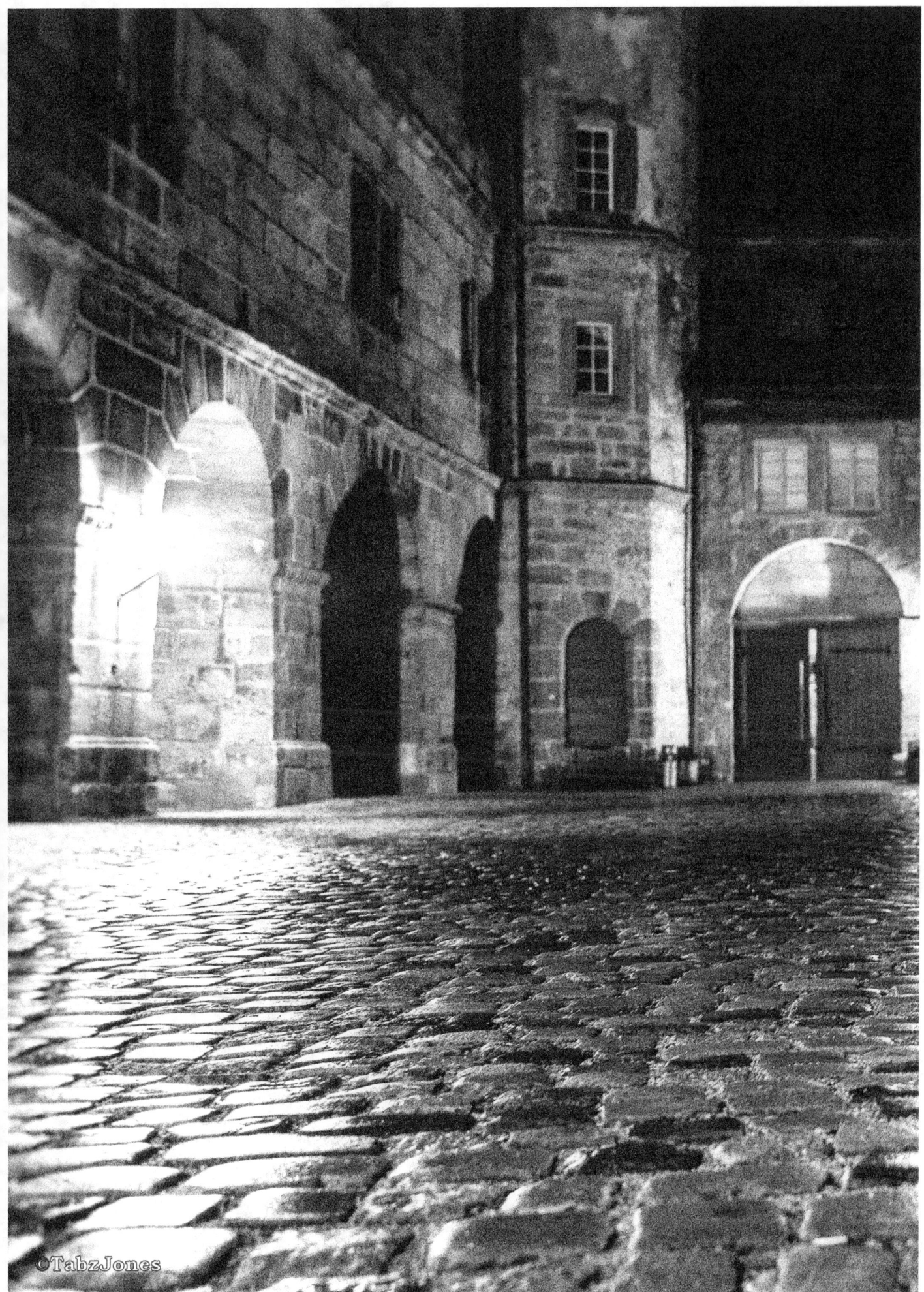

©TabzJones

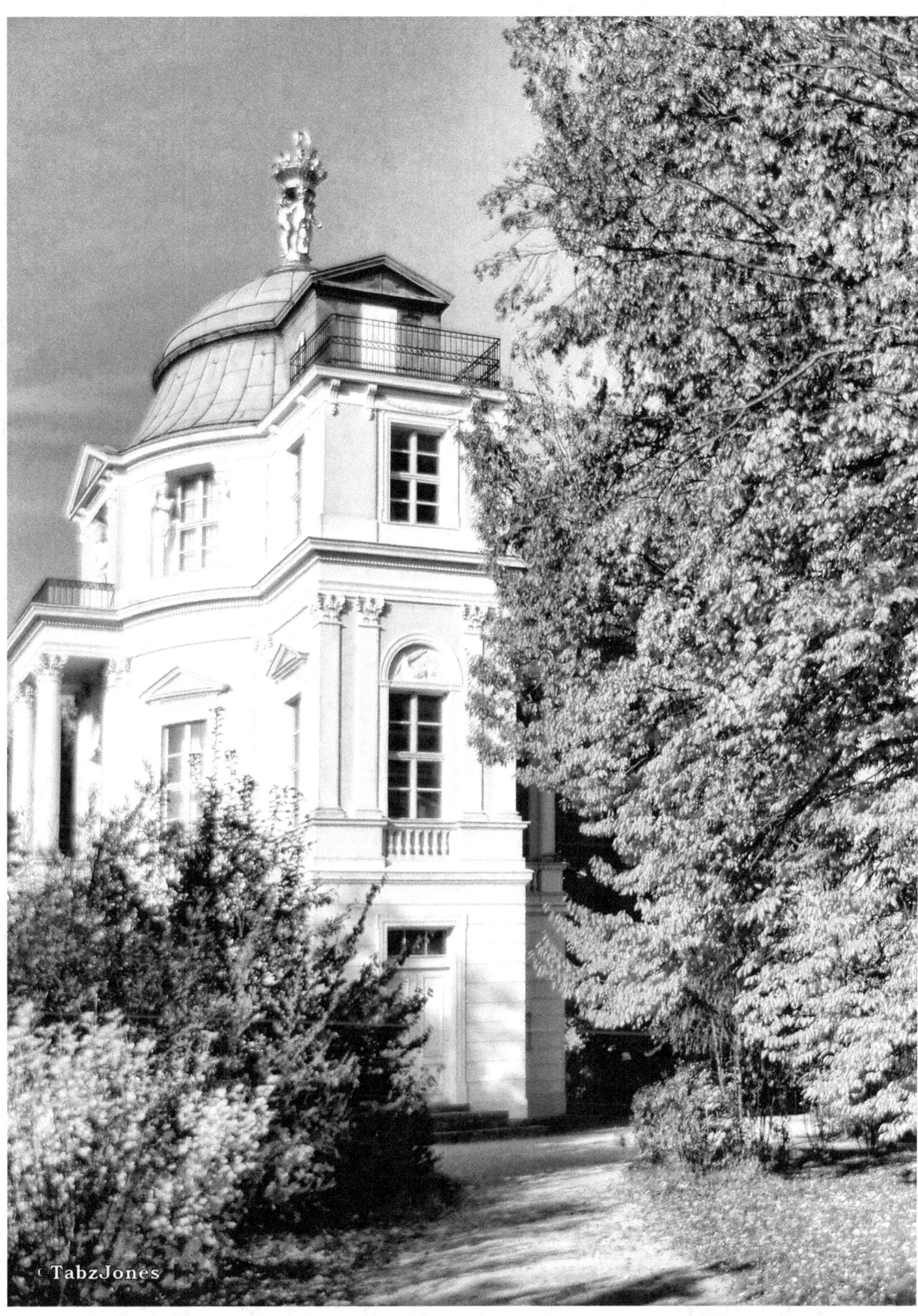

© TabzJones

www.ingramcontent.com/pod-product-compliance
Lightning Source LLC
Chambersburg PA
CBHW081305180526
45170CB00007B/2568